YORK NOTES

Cider with Rosie

Laurie Lee

Note by Julian Choyce

 Longman   York Press

Julian Choyce is hereby identified as author of this work in accordance with
Section 77 of the Copyright, Designs and Patents Act 1988

YORK PRESS
322 Old Brompton Road, London SW5 9JH

PEARSON EDUCATION LIMITED
Edinburgh Gate, Harlow,
Essex CM20 2JE, United Kingdom
Associated companies, branches and representatives throughout the world

First published 1999

ISBN 0–582–36823–5

Designed by Vicki Pacey
Illustrated by Stephen Player
Phototypeset by Gem Graphics, Trenance, Mawgan Porth, Cornwall
Colour reproduction and film output by Spectrum Colour
Produced by Addison Wesley Longman China Limited, Hong Kong

CONTENTS

PREFACE

York Notes are designed to give you a broader perspective on works of literature studied at GCSE and equivalent levels. We have carried out extensive research into the needs of the modern literature student prior to publishing this new edition. Our research showed that no existing series fully met students' requirements. Rather than present a single authoritative approach, we have provided alternative viewpoints, empowering students to reach their own interpretations of the text. York Notes provide a close examination of the work and include biographical and historical background, summaries, glossaries, analyses of characters, themes, structure and language, cultural connections and literary terms.

If you look at the Contents page you will see the structure for the series. However, there's no need to read from the beginning to the end as you would with a novel, play, poem or short story. Use the Notes in the way that suits you. Our aim is to help you with your understanding of the work, not to dictate how you should learn.

York Notes are written by English teachers and examiners, with an expert knowledge of the subject. They show you how to succeed in coursework and examination assignments, guiding you through the text and offering practical advice. Questions and comments will extend, test and reinforce your knowledge. Attractive colour design and illustrations improve clarity and understanding, making these Notes easy to use and handy for quick reference.

York Notes are ideal for:
- Essay writing
- Exam preparation
- Class discussion

The author of this Note is Julian Choyce, who studied English at the New University of Ulster and Reading. He was born in Gloucester and has taught both in Britain and overseas, preparing students for public examinations at all levels. He is an assistant examiner in English for a major GCSE examination board.

The edition used in this Note is Penguin Books edition, with drawings by John Ward, 1962.

Health Warning: **This study guide will enhance your understanding, but should not replace the reading of the original text and/or study in class.**

PART ONE

INTRODUCTION

HOW TO STUDY A NOVEL

You have bought this book because you wanted to study a novel on your own. This may supplement classwork.

- You will need to read the novel several times. Start by reading it quickly for pleasure, then read it slowly and carefully. Further readings will generate new ideas and help you to memorise the details of the story.
- Make careful notes on themes, plot and characters of the novel. The plot will change some of the characters. Who changes?
- The novel may not present events chronologically. Does the novel you are reading begin at the beginning of the story or does it contain flashbacks and a muddled time sequence? Can you think why?
- How is the story told? Is it narrated by one of the characters or by an all-seeing ('omniscient') narrator?
- Does the same person tell the story all the way through? Or do we see the events through the minds and feelings of a number of different people.
- Which characters does the narrator like? Which characters do you like or dislike? Do your sympathies change during the course of the book? Why? When?
- Any piece of writing (including your notes and essays) is the result of thousands of choices. No book had to be written in just one way: the author could have chosen other words, other phrases, other characters, other events. How could the author of your novel have written the story differently? If events were recounted by a minor character how would this change the novel?

Studying on your own requires self-discipline and a carefully thought-out work plan in order to be effective. Good luck.

LAURIE LEE'S BACKGROUND

Biographical details

How are his feelings about his father made clear in the story?

Laurie Lee was born in the town of Stroud in Gloucestershire on 26 June 1914. At the age of three his father, Reg Lee, abandoned his family in search of a career as a civil servant in London. Circumstances forced Laurie Lee's mother to rent a small cottage in the nearby village of Slad, which is where the writer's **autobiography** (see Literary Terms) begins.

Laurie Lee attended the local village school and later Stroud Central School.

In his teens, a succession of dreary jobs encouraged the youngster to seek adventure. In 1934 he left the valley in which he had been brought up and after a spell in London as a labourer embarked on a journey to Spain. He travelled mainly on foot, busking for money with a violin or taking offers of casual work. When Civil War broke out in 1936 he was rescued, along with other British citizens, by a navy warship.

During the Second World War Laurie Lee worked for the ministry of information, in their film unit.

In 1950 he married his wife Catherine. He was forty-nine years old when their daughter Jersey was born. In 1952 he was awarded the MBE.

Cider with Rosie was published in 1959. It begins with a note that 'some of the facts may be distorted by time', but events closely follow the author's upbringing in the West Country of England.

Consider the extent to which this is an account of the author's life or the community in which he lived.

The success of *Cider with Rosie* enabled Laurie Lee to return to Slad and buy property there, even the cricket ground in Sheepscombe where Uncle Sid had astonished the author with bat and ball.

Later Laurie Lee fought on behalf of the village of Slad to preserve the valley from a large housing development.

In 1997 Laurie Lee died at his home, aged 82. He was buried in the village churchyard beside the tiny church where he had sung as a boy in the choir. A brass plaque bears his name above his favourite spot in the Woolpack pub.

His work identifies strongly with rural life, and in depicting the valley of his upbringing he succeeds in preserving it.

Other works

Laurie Lee claimed that he had written 'little that was not for the most part autobiographical'. *Cider with Rosie* was published in 1959 and details the writer's childhood and early teens. It was acclaimed worldwide and became a popular text in schools.

Two other titles follow it. *As I Walked Out One Midsummer Morning* (1969) is an account of the writer's travels. In the 1930s Laurie Lee, like many other unemployed men, was forced to look farther afield for work. Laurie Lee describes a journey that took him first to London and later to Spain and back again.

Later Laurie Lee returned to Spain and his book entitled *A Rose for Winter* (1955) charts his experiences in Andalusia.

A collection of short extracts and essays entitled *I Can't Stay Long* (1975) makes useful reading. In the essay 'Writing Autobiography' he reflects on the decisions he made in selecting and shaping his memories for *Cider with Rosie*.

How is his skill as a poet apparent in the style of his prose writing?

Much of Laurie Lee's poetry and prose work focuses on personal experience and has an extraordinarily strong sense of time and place.

Four volumes of poetry, *The Sun My Monument* (1944), *The Bloom of Candles* (1947), *My Many Coated Man* (1955) and *Pocket Poems* (1960), explore themes related to Laurie Lee's varied experiences.

War

Laurie Lee was born in June 1914. Later that year the First World War broke out in Europe. It would end just as the child might begin to be aware of such things.

Consider how appropriate it is that the story of a country boy who outgrows his rural background should be set alongside reflections on quite major changes to the world he inhabits.

Whilst Laurie Lee, the toddler, grapples with the geography of house and garden, his uncles, those distant 'khaki ghosts' who appear occasionally on leave, exhausted, are fighting at the Front in France.

Two of them, Sid and Charlie, survived an earlier conflict in South Africa; the Boer War ended in 1902.

By the end of the first chapter it is 1918. The war is over and there are raucous celebrations in the village, but the pioneering uncles on horseback return to a changing world.

After the war

The motor car gradually replaces the horse; the charabanc replaces the wagon. The 1920s saw the advent of radio and suddenly the village was no longer isolated. The Industrial Revolution had created factories, industries and changing patterns of work. The order and the authority of the Church and the Squire were now challenged by new ideas and the world outside. Life no longer revolved around the agricultural calendar.

Although Laurie Lee points out that change 'came late' (p. 00) to the secluded valley of his boyhood, its effect was nevertheless devastating.

The world Laurie Lee describes is somehow frozen in the past, peaceful, slow and uncomplicated. Villages are no longer quite like that.

Setting

Notice how the author is affected by his peaceful upbringing.

It would be naïve to idealise the **setting** (see Literary Terms) as it is depicted in the story. In many ways Laurie Lee's upbringing is harsh and confined. Poor diet and basic living conditions account for the childhood illnesses he suffered, and to which many fell victim, including his sister.

As you read through the story think about how many people have lives of frustrated ambitions. It would also be useful to think about whether the world of Laurie Lee's childhood offers a sense of fulfilment that is missing from the world we live in today.

We can understand the writer's yearnings to escape but also the sense of loyalty and affection for the place he grew up in.

PART TWO

SUMMARIES

GENERAL SUMMARY

Chapter 1:
Earliest
memories

Laurie Lee is three years old when the story starts. His mother, sisters Marjorie, Dorothy and Phyllis, and brothers Jack, Tony and Harold arrive at a small rented cottage in the village of Slad in Gloucestershire. It is the summer of 1918 and news of the end of the First World War is as bewildering as the author's new surroundings.

Chapters 2–4:
Local life

With the help of his family Laurie Lee is quickly acquainted with the more colourful characters found in the village from time to time. Cabbage-Stump Charlie and Albert the Devil are to be feared, as is Jones's Goat. Percy-from-Painswick and Willy the Fish are less comical than sad.

Winter weather throws the household into chaos. Their cottage with its steep garden is prone to flooding.

At school Laurie Lee enjoys the cosy atmosphere of the infant class but must come to terms with more demanding lessons in the juniors. His teachers are the patient Miss Wardley and the fearsome Miss B.

Separated from her husband, their mother struggles to cope, but despite poor and often cramped conditions, they share a happy home life.

Chapters
5–10: Family
and relatives

In a separate part of the house, Granny Trill and Granny Wallon are sworn enemies until the death of Granny Trill ends their feud.

Laurie Lee learns of death from stories and incidents in the history of the village. There is the suicide of lonely Miss Flynn, discovered drowned in a local pond. The strange tale of a villager's return from New Zealand and his subsequent murder is a lesson for the child in village life and loyalties.

Laurie Lee accompanies his mother on visits to the elderly and infirm. At home she tells the children stories from her own past, largely spent caring for others – most notably the family left in her charge by the husband who deserted her.

Throughout the year Laurie Lee and his friends live an active outdoor life but the author was once prone to illness and came close to death himself at an early age.

Periodic visits from their uncles, Tom, Sid, Charlie and Ray, with stories of faraway places and distant conflicts alert the children to the wider world.

Chapters 11–12: Growing up

In the face of hardship the village enjoy lively get-togethers. At the end of the First World War a fancy dress parade and procession end with speeches and photographs in the grounds of the Squires house.

The church choir organise a charabanc outing to the seaside town of Weston-super-Mare and in winter locals gather at the village school for The Parochial Church Tea and Annual Entertainments: a series of sketches, songs and comic turns.

Now in his early teens Laurie Lee begins to change his opinion of girls. Jo is a classmate and girlfriend. Later an encounter with the older and more experienced Rosie Burdock represents for the author, a coming of age.

Chapter 13: Changes

Life in the village, unaltered for thousands of years, finally exhibits the symptoms of change. Laurie Lee's own family begins to fragment as his sisters find boyfriends and eventually husbands. The author's mother is older and Laurie Lee is now a young man.

CHAPTER 1 – FIRST LIGHT

When we meet Laurie Lee he is just three years old. It is June 1918. The Lee family have arrived in the village of Slad in Gloucestershire and Laurie is deposited from the carriers cart that brought them, onto the grassy bank that falls down towards the cottage they will rent.

Gradually Laurie Lee takes in his new surroundings while the rest of the family unload their belongings and make the cottage habitable.

What do you notice about the way in which the author's sisters are described?

At the end of a hectic first day the Lees' family home has taken shape and its often chaotic but vibrant nature will be central to the story of Laurie's early life.

As time passes Laurie Lee's curiosity extends to a study of the house, the knots in the boarded ceiling and the delights to be sampled from the family vegetable garden.

One morning, on waking, Laurie Lee is outraged to find his eyes glued tight shut. His sisters are quick to reassure him that this is only the 'sweet glue of sleep'.

More surprises follow when he is amazed to see leaves falling from the trees outside. Again, the girls are on hand to explain that it is now autumn and the trees are not 'falling to bits'.

When a strange man visits the house one morning, wet and miserable from sleeping rough in the nearby woods, we guess from his mothers questions that the man has somehow escaped the fighting in France. Laurie Lee's brothers and sisters view with horror and fascination. For Laurie it is an uncomfortable glimpse of the First World War, of which his relatives are a part.

With the onset of winter comes news that the war has ended. Laurie Lee's mother has gone to visit his father, noticeable by his absence in this opening section.

Laurie and his sisters walk through the village after dark and view the celebrations. With his mother gone and the war over, it seems to Laurie as if the whole world has ended.

COMMENT   In this opening chapter the author's memory extends back as far as he is able. In this sense the house and its surroundings feel like the place where his character was born. Several references on pages 13 and 14 refer to this arrival as a kind of birth: 'it was the beginning of a life'.

The surroundings are described in a way that is rich, even tropical. The language of these early descriptions is full of **imagery** (see Literary Terms). The grassy bank on which Laurie Lee finds himself (p. 9) is so foreign to him that it is not inappropriate for Lee to describe it as if it were a jungle.

Notice how cleverly Lee adopts a child's perspective and asks us to experience events using the senses of a small boy. The peculiar description of what it feels and sounds like to submerge one's head in a bucket of water (p. 15) is an excellent example. In the confusion of moving house we view the chaos amid a forest of legs (see Theme on Growing Up).

The narrow world of house and valley are the whole world to the young writer. Laurie Lee often uses the language of geography to map the child's broadening horizons. The yard outside is as vast as an ocean (p. 16).

Moments of wry humour add to the story's appeal. The older writer enjoys recalling the strange objects that might appear in a loaf of bread (p. 16) in the days of 'happy go lucky baking'.

See how the style of **narrative** (see Literary Terms) can be used for different effects. Laurie Lee's partial understanding when the strange visitor appears (p. 20), snippets of eavesdropping dialogue and carefully selected details (torn khaki and medals), help to build the sense of mystery and suspense. We are offered glimpses of a more serious, adult world in a tantalising way.

Note how events outside the valley take time to impact on the daily life of the village.

When Laurie Lee is unrolled from a Union Jack (p. 10) to take his place in the village, we are reminded that his story and that of the community represent a living piece in a very English history. Later, in fancy dress, Laurie Lee appears as a young John Bull (p. 186).

GLOSSARY   **carrier's cart** horse-drawn wagon

TEST YOURSELF (CHAPTER 1)

 Identify the characters.

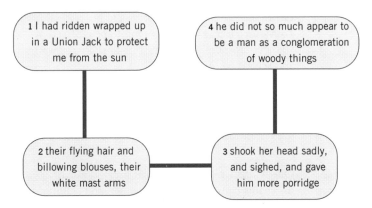

1 I had ridden wrapped up in a Union Jack to protect me from the sun

4 he did not so much appear to be a man as a conglomeration of woody things

2 their flying hair and billowing blouses, their white mast arms

3 shook her head sadly, and sighed, and gave him more porridge

Identify the person 'to whom' this comment refers.

5 I confused him with the Kaiser. Would he die now the war was over?

Check your answers on page 77.

 Consider these issues.

a How the writer encourages us to see the world as a child does.

b The way nature is used in descriptions.

c The role his sisters play in Laurie Lee's upbringing.

d How we are made aware of a child's growing experience.

e Early indications of his mother's character.

f The author's father and his feelings about him.

g Laurie Lee's feelings at the end of the chapter.

Chapter 2 – First Names

Peace brings little to alter day-to-day life for Laurie. His mother returns from her visit to her husband. Laurie Lee learns that he is soon to be replaced by younger brother Tony as the one to share the warmth and security of his mother's bed.

His attention now turns to other beings, both real and imagined. He pictures demons beyond the village, stalking him, and his sisters enjoy scaring him with tales of the 'Old Men' (p. 28) who may lurk about the house.

How does the writer build a sense of tension and suspense in this section?

One winter's night Jones's goat breaks loose dragging his chains behind him while women and children take cover.

Other phenomena include a two-headed sheep said to talk to passers-by and the ghostly Bulls Cross Coach. Some villagers claim to have seen or heard the ghost of a stagecoach that crashed one night. Others fear the curse that falls upon those who brag of a sighting. This bleak crossroads at the head of the valley is a place of violence, both past and present. A gibbet had stood there and locals were naturally wary of the place.

The wood known as Deadcombe Bottom excites the child's imagination too. Here lived the hangman for the gallows at Bulls Cross. The crumbled remains of his cottage in the wood are a popular playground for the village children. The circumstances of the Hangman's death soon became a subject of fascination, as did the accidental murder of his son. The hook where the Hangman hung himself up can be found in the old walls of the cottage.

Now aged five, Laurie recalls other prominent characters from village life. Cabbage-Stump Charlie is an aggressive neighbour to be avoided where possible. Percy-from-Painswick entertains the local girls with his colourful antics. Others include Albert the Devil, Willy the Fish, Prospect Smiler, John-Jack and Emmanuel Twinning (see Characters).

Note your early impressions of the writer's mother. With the summer of 1921 comes serious drought. Whilst the neighbours pray for rain or shoot 'at passing clouds' (p. 37), the Lees fear the inevitable downpour. Their cottage lies on a steep incline at the mercy of a flood. One stormy night their mother wakes the family. Armed with brooms, frantic attempts to stem the flood ensue. When the crisis is over his mother's curses hint at difficulties she faces raising two families single-handedly.

The older author still feels uneasy whenever rain threatens.

COMMENT   In this section we begin to see the ways in which Laurie Lee's character will be shaped by relationships in his early life. His mother will have a profound and positive effect on him (see Characters). Already he senses the complexity of relationships. Ousted from his mother's bed he feels 'the gentle, merciless rejection of women' (p. 28).

The image of the Bulls Cross Coach is a very potent one and excites the young boy's imagination. A picture of the broken carriage, 'the sobbing horses kicking out each others brains' (p. 33), haunts him in a way that is more immediate and terrible than the recent war.

Other stories are told with similar skill and economy. We are reminded of the author's taste for the macabre. The story of the Bulls Cross Hangman is both stark and tragic. Other lives in the story will be enacted with similar poignancy and simplicity.

Laurie Lee is also quick to pay respect to the vitality of the living; life goes on. So it is quite natural in the author's eyes for the children to 'swing from that dead hook' in the Hangman's ruined cottage and kick 'the damp walls to pieces' (p. 34).

Laurie Lee has a sensitive ear for local dialect. 'They sin that coach agen … 'Arry Lazbury sin it, they says' (p. 33). Snippets of dialogue in broad Gloucestershire accents help to elaborate on the story. The novelist and poet Thomas Hardy uses a similar technique in his tales of Dorset. This **rustic chorus** (see Literary Terms) also adds drama to events; we hear what onlookers may have said, as if they were ourselves.

Which parts of this story do you find comical to read?

Dialogue can be used for other effects. Jones's goat stalks the village like a god (p. 31) but this legend loses its impact with time and the reflections of Laurie Lee's sisters.

Often the writer is amused by gossip and how comically the local's trade in it. The two-headed sheep belongs to village folklore. Laurie Lee comments wryly that 'few, naturally enough, had seen it' (p. 32). Those who told tales of the ghostly coach (p. 33) would die a terrible death. 'So', says the writer, 'news of the phantom usually came second-hand' (p. 33).

Laurie Lee prefers **images** (see Literary Terms) drawn from the natural world he knows. He clings to the sleeping body of his mother 'snug as a mouse in a hayrick' (p. 27).

'First Names' offers a broad cross-section of village life from comic to tragic, but all are dramatised from the wide-eyed perspective of a child.

GLOSSARY   **gibbet/gallows**   scaffolding on which criminals were hanged

CHAPTER **3** – VILLAGE SCHOOL

The chapter opens with a description of the valley itself. It is a place that seems cut off from the world outside. Within the valley lies a scattering of thirty or so Cotswold buildings, among them a small village school.

How does humour contribute to our enjoyment of this section?

Laurie Lee is about to follow his brothers and sisters through the school's two classes. Reluctant to attend at all, Laurie Lee's first day is a bruising and bewildering experience, but he is soon at home in the rough and tumble of the playground. His child-like honesty and sense of enquiry lead to inevitable punishments but the gentle pace and security of the infants are to the writer's liking.

A harsher regime is to follow when Laurie Lee graduates to the Big Room, and experiences the rigid discipline of Miss Crabby B. who terrorises her classes, until Spadge Hopkins, a fellow pupil challenges her authority and wins (see Characters).

Miss Wardley from Birmingham, whose methods are direct but her expectations realistic, replaces Miss B (see Characters).

In the meantime, for Laurie Lee's generation, school means time when they are deprived of the world outside. An account of a day's events follows. Excusing himself from class the writer dreams boyishly of the bright future he may have.

At break-time furtive comments passed over the wall at the girls on the other side are the first clumsy attempts at relations with the other sex.

A range of characters populates the school yard: Jo and Poppy – his 'girlfriends' from the infants, Walt Kerry the bully, loud Bill Timbrell, the Ballingers, Browns and Betty Gleed (see Characters).

Back in class dreary lessons are interrupted by visits from the Squire with prizes and the occasional beating (see Characters). The children use their ingenuity in inventing excuses for avoiding lessons, and the school succeeds in tempering their innate distrust of outsiders and their other prejudices; when the gypsy Rosso steals food because he is hungry and is beaten, he wins the approval of his classmates.

At age fourteen Laurie Lee is free to leave. He and his peers have learnt all they were likely to ask for and are shrewd enough to realise that Miss Wardley's invitations for them to visit are rather hollow.

COMMENT   Look more closely at the description of the valley (p. 41). The writer traces its origins back to the ice age and remnants like 'Roman snails' suggest a vast time scale in a place where little has changed. So rare and isolated is the **setting** (see Literary Terms) that curious properties in the water endow the village women with their own beauty.

However, Laurie Lee is quick to remind us of life's limitations. Economics for a typical household is a stark choice between the land, the Squire or factory work (see Context and Setting). 'Honey'-coloured Cotswold cottages may be quaint and pretty but at the rear their vegetable plots are 'insurance against hard times' (p. 42).

Does the writer feel his education was worthwhile?

What is on offer at the village school is equally narrow. Direct comments from the author are for you to interpret. How does the writer feel about instruction that provided 'no more than was needed to measure a shed' or 'read a swine-disease warning'? (p. 53).

Ambivalent feelings in the writer's mind make this section fascinating reading. Portraits of the teachers are sharply focused and range from comic revulsion to tender respect. In the end the writer admits that despite the schools poverty and overcrowding he 'relished it' (p. 53).

Do you think these accounts of school life are realistic or nostalgic impressions.

One passage in particular stands out. The writer shifts into the present tense (p. 53) to give the classroom, with its drowsy chants, and the boisterous activity of the playground, a quite vivid intensity (see Theme on Growing Up). Lists of sights, sounds and sensations evoke powerfully both the world of the schoolroom and of childhood. 'We all double up; we can't speak for laughing, we can't laugh without hitting each other' (p. 55).

CHAPTER 4 – THE KITCHEN

The writer now expands upon sparse references to the father that deserted them. Five children survive from his father's previous marriage and three more follow when he marries his housekeeper; Laurie's own mother.

List the details that depict their father in a poor light.

At the age of three Laurie Lee's father left for London and never returned. We are left to guess what the author's feelings about him may be.

The sisters encountered earlier are fleshed out more fully too. Marjorie, Dorothy and Phyllis are half-sisters by his father's earlier marriage; their real mother died young.

Marjorie, the eldest, is like a second mother to Laurie Lee. She takes a share of responsibility within the household and the author comments on her unconscious grace and beauty. Dorothy is lively and alert to gossip, whilst Phyllis is grave but protective in her attentions to her younger brothers (see Characters).

Reggie and Harold are half-brothers, Harold living with them and Reggie elsewhere. Jack and Tony are the writer's real brothers. He appears closest to Jack, the oldest of the three, Tony being the youngest and the odd one out (see Characters).

Conditions are cramped but the family co-exists happily. A typical day revolves around the kitchen. Breakfast is a haphazard affair as their mother struggles to feed the family in time for school or work. The girls set off for work in Stroud (see Context and Setting). *How does life in the Lee household compare with your own?* The boys will spend their free time avoiding their mother's errands. The evening meal gathers the family together again and is equally chaotic. The boys are perpetually hungry. Later they all amuse themselves and each other. Laurie Lee's mother presides over the fire or busies herself in cutting extracts from the newspaper. The children play, draw or tell stories. All tolerate the 'slashing and scrapings' (p. 00) of Laurie Lee's violin practice. This is the time when the day's news is shared. The girls gossip and the warm range and drone of voices make him drowsy. His sisters carry him up to his bedroom. The room is cold but he is soon asleep.

COMMENT   In his essay 'Writing Autobiography' (1975) Laurie Lee describes the difficulties of selecting material from the clutter of childhood experiences. Commenting on his schooling he explains, 'Here five thousand hours had to be reduced to fifteen minutes ... and those fifteen minutes, without wearying the reader, must seem like five thousand hours'. Descriptions of the family home work in a similar way. What we are left with are details that form an overall impression of family life with the warmth and security of the kitchen at its heart (see Theme on Growing Up). At times the character of Laurie Lee himself recedes into the background; a presence that watches, listens and records.

How does the lack of any 'male authority' (p. 60) affect the author?

Notice the prominence of his mother and sisters in the author's upbringing. This is what he refers to when he describes the 'rule of women' in their cottage (p. 60).

A clearer picture of the writer's mother emerges (see Characters). Small details are significant. There's 'no method' (p. 69) to mealtimes, she mislays the matches and sends the boys on errands having forgotten to buy things (p. 68). However her 'unreasoning' (p. 61) loyalty to husband and family, her exuberance and encouragement are the things that the author remembers most.

Look at the way the writer uses **irony** (see Literary Terms) to hint at feelings about his father's lack of concern. Read closely, and the account that opens this section describes a cold and rather selfish man (p. 60).

GLOSSARY   **range** cast iron fireplace for cooking

A *Identify the characters.*

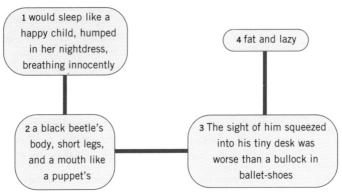

1 would sleep like a happy child, humped in her nightdress, breathing innocently

4 fat and lazy

2 a black beetle's body, short legs, and a mouth like a puppet's

3 The sight of him squeezed into his tiny desk was worse than a bullock in ballet-shoes

Identify the person 'to whom' this comment refers.

5 a blonde Aphrodite, appeared quite unconscious of the rarity of herself

Check your answers on page 77.

B *Consider these issues.*

a How peace affects young Laurie Lee's early life.

b The effect of stories about local characters on the young author.

c The part played by rumour and gossip in village life.

d How the writer feels about the education he received.

e The way in which the writer presents his father to us.

f How the family spend the time they have together in the evenings.

g The quite different descriptions of the three sisters.

CHAPTER 5 – GRANNIES IN THE WAINSCOT

Granny Trill and Granny Wallen are tenants in the rented cottage shared by the Lee family. With their 'sickle-bent bodies' (p. 78) the two old ladies live separately, one above the other and are fierce enemies.

Granny Wallen lives downstairs and occupies her time among the hedgerows collecting ingredients for her potent wines. She is poor but rumoured to be of noble blood.

What is their mother's reaction to the children's mockery?

Granny Trill lives 'Up-Atop' (p. 78). She chews incessantly and the boys enjoy doing impressions of her. Her vices are snuff and the almanac she keeps hooked on the wall. Her upbringing as a woodsman's daughter occupies part of this section, as does the death of her father, skewered by a falling tree. He had planted the seed of the large Beech in the garden and jealously guarded his beautiful daughter from male callers.

When Laurie Lee's sisters decide to dress up and entertain Granny Trill, their home-made attempts at fashion and finery offend the old lady. 'Aping the gentry' (p. 91) is a sin according to her upbringing.

Aware of each other's comings and goings these two 'rival ancients' keep a rigid timetable that ensures they never meet, preferring to communicate with brooms on ceilings and boots on floors.

Eventually, Granny Trill breaks her hip and dies and their enmity appears to be over, until Granny Wallen's commotion at the funeral. She is incensed at the age engraved on the coffin; 'a lie ... ain't more'n ninety, an' I gone on ninety-two'. (p. 93)

Ironically these two elderly ladies 'like cold twin stars' had more in common than they knew. With her enemy gone Granny Wallen barely survives two weeks before joining her.

COMMENT   The lives and deaths of both old ladies underline the twin themes of time and change (see Theme on Time and Change). Both share an 'original sense of time' (p. 82); Granny Trill is comforted by the tick of her clock, the hands, we are told, had 'fallen off years ago'. Granny Wallen's wine making is governed by the seasons.

Can we guess at what Granny Trill and Granny Wallen think of Laurie Lee's family?

Their rigid codes of behaviour belong to the past and are under threat of change. Their elaborate dress for outings amuses the children (p. 87), but to dress inappropriately is to ignore one's class; one's station and risk shame (p. 91).

The grannies' story plots the end of generations and traditions. No one can verify Granny Trill's real age within the village because quite simply 'there was no one old enough to know' (p. 93).

GLOSSARY   **snuff** powdered tobacco, sniffed up nostril

almanac book of astrological charts and predictions

CHAPTER 6 – PUBLIC DEATH, PRIVATE MURDER

The writer now recalls a strange and violent event that took place shortly after the end of the First World War. A young man appears at the local pub on a bitter winter evening. It is Christmas time. Leaving the valley for New Zealand he has made his fortune and has returned to surprise his family. He spreads a wad of notes along the bar and pulls out an expensive watch for the assembled company to admire. The men folk accept his drinks and allow themselves to be taunted at their lack of adventure. When the visitor settles up and heads off into the blizzards a group of men follow. He is beaten and kicked and left to freeze to death.

How does the
writer tempt us to
take the villagers'
side in this story?

Police investigations lead nowhere until the ramblings of an old lady on her deathbed mention a gold watch and appear to implicate her sons. When she dies the village's secret goes with her.

The suicide of Miss Flynn leaves a deep impression on the author. She seems kind and distracted to the children and the villagers are shocked when Fred Bates finds her naked body drowned in Jones's pond.

Freezing winters claim the lives of many of the village's older inhabitants. Laurie Lee recalls vividly the sight of old Mr Davies on his deathbed.

Joseph and Hannah Brown are the perfect couple, content to live out their time in their cottage near the common. When they become too frail to take care of each other and are banished to separate wings of the Workhouse they are found dead within a week.

COMMENT

The stories in this section tend toward a similar purpose. Authority is a concept that somehow belongs elsewhere. The villagers themselves share their own peculiar and ancient sense of what is right and wrong (p. 104). Vincent's boasts of a better life elsewhere offend those who have remained loyal to the valley (see Theme on Village Life). Ironically he meets his death at the spot of the old gallows and when the police arrive the villagers quickly close ranks to protect the guilty.

Laurie Lee blames faceless authority for the death of the Browns. The Workhouse ensures that their lives cannot reach a natural conclusion together, however pitiful. Even the abandoned cottage registers their outrage. 'Its decay was so violent and overwhelming, it was as though the old couple had wrecked it themselves' (p. 111).

The stories are also unified by their effect on the child. Violent images and the 'sharp death-taste' remain with the author. For example:

- The pond he revisits, that had choked Miss Flynn
- The face of Albert Davies, 'a skull wrapped in yellow paper'
- A murder scene at Bulls Cross, 'the indignant blood in the snow'

GLOSSARY   **workhouse** place that housed poor people of the parish

CHAPTER *7* – MOTHER

Laurie Lee's mother grew up in Quedgeley in Gloucester. She was the daughter of John Light, a coachman. She is portrayed as a popular girl with a lively mind. At school her teacher encourages her but her education is cut short when she must nurse her ailing mother.

As a young woman she becomes a maid to the gentry. She later entertains Laurie Lee and the children with tales of the 'Big House'. Her recollections are often exotic or romantic, meeting an Indian Prince during her days of domestic service or admiring looks from the soldiers at Aldershot on her Sundays off.

What aspects of Mrs Lee's character might make her a difficult partner?

After a brief spell as a country barmaid she answers an advertisement for a housekeeper. She promptly falls in love with her employer, Laurie Lee's father. She is forced to uproot herself and the children to Slad when he eventually leaves her, and dreamily recalls those early years of her marriage as the happiest of her life.

Without their father, the family lives a turbulent life. Their mother is an extreme and buoyant character despite debts and frustrated ambitions. Laurie Lee recalls the embarrassment of having to keep busloads of people waiting while his mother searched for her gloves, or their chaotic house crammed with her bargains from sales and auctions.

Her love of music and knowledge of finer things are a part of her nature as are the darker moments when she dwells on the husband who left her and the four year old daughter who died (p. 135).

Her time is her own when the family eventually leave, but she welcomes their visits without fuss or ceremony (p. 135).

She had remained loyal to her husband for thirty-five years. When news of his death reaches her she gives up hope and is buried alongside her infant daughter.

COMMENT

Consider to what extent their mother has sacrificed her own ambitions for her children.

If we have grown used to an account of the young writer's early experiences, this section begins to outgrow that time frame. His mother's entire life, spanning her childhood, hopes, frustrations and eventual death, has been compressed into one remarkable account. Think about how this succeeds in reinforcing the theme of time and change.

CHAPTER **8** – WINTER AND SUMMER

Harsh winters stick in the writer's mind. During the freeze, even the church clock and weathercock are motionless. For Laurie Lee and his young friends there is always plenty to do. Armed with cocoa tins filled with smouldering rags they gather in the lane and punch each other or play 'giddy up' to keep warm (p. 138). Sometimes they help out at the farm feeding cattle. Often they join their school friends skating on Jones's pond. When snow comes and fills the lanes the villagers are unconcerned. They'd 'been cut off before, after all' (p. 142).

Which details are most memorable when the Squire is described?

At Christmas time carol singing is one of the church choir's 'perks'. First stop is the Squire's house whose generous two shillings set a precedent for others to compete with. They reserve the final song for the aptly named Joseph whose farm is the last house high on the hill.

Summers are as sudden as they are extreme. In the author's memory it seemed an endless time when nothing much happened. The adults complain about the heat. The children are free to roam the dusty lane, chew grass, suck sherbet, or join in boisterous games like ducking pigeons with Sixpence Robinson and her brothers and sisters (see Characters).

There are games of cricket or picnics to occupy the long days, and in the evenings the children have the village to themselves for games like 'Fox and Hounds'.

COMMENT

The role of nature in ordering the villagers' lives is the subject of this section. The seemingly aimless activities of the children are somehow dictated by the seasons, as they have been for generations. Clocks stop and winds are 'stilled' in winter. In summer the moon governs their play (p. 153).

The Squire makes another brief appearance. Tradition ensures that the carol singers call on the 'Big House' first but his frailty reminds us of his dwindling influence in village affairs (see Context and Setting).

Descriptions of the two seasons are charged with emotion. Details may be realistic – the pain as cold hands thaw out (p. 141) – but how far are different times of the year idealised by the writer?

CHAPTER 9 – SICK BOY

As an infant Laurie Lee was prone to illness. So much so that he boasts of having being christened twice; hurriedly at birth when his mother feared he would die and again three years later. In his first year he suffers a series of illnesses and at eighteen months, during the birth of his brother Tony, a helpful neighbour mistakenly prepares him for burial when pneumonia strikes a second time.

What are the author's feelings about the loss of his sister?

Sadly Frances, the author's sister, is less fortunate and dies at the age of four.

Although Laurie Lee appeared robust enough and was treated as such, periodic fits and fevers follow him throughout his childhood. In his sick bed he imagines he were a king with anxious subjects awaiting his recovery. As fever takes hold he might see visions, hear voices or become delirious himself.

Whilst the family become familiar with these bouts of illness and the author enjoys a form of celebrity status as a result, he later recognises the seriousness of his symptoms. Tuberculosis and Pneumonia accounted for scores of infant deaths.

Laurie Lee recalls waking one night and calmly surveying the worried faces of his family at his bedside (p. 153) but he was not averse to faking his symptoms to avoid unpleasant medicine too (p. 165).

FAMILY AND RELATIVES

Repeated recovery from fever convince him of his 'toughness', give him a fresh appetite for life and afford him the luxuries of convalescence; his mother's renewed affections, 'a paint-box. And maybe some liquorice allsorts' (p. 167).

In later life the writer claims to hear voices in his head from a collision with a cyclist and concussion as a child.

COMMENT   Laurie Lee's precarious health as a child underlines the realities of his upbringing. The story predates the National Health Service. Fortunately Laurie Lee is nursed back to health but Frances, his sister dies 'An ignorant death which need never have happened' (p. 157). We are also reminded of other deaths in the family. 'My father had buried three of his children already' (p. 156).

Frequent illness shapes the character of the child. On his recovery Laurie Lee's sensations are heightened and every day things become suddenly precious to him (pp. 160–2).

CHAPTER 10 – THE UNCLES

Laurie Lee wastes little time on Uncle George, his father's brother and 'a rogue'. His Uncle Fred sold insurance and moved away. However his other Uncles are adventurers and heroes in the author's young eyes.

John Light the coachman had five sons, Charlie, Tom, Ray, Sid and Fred (see Characters). Uncle Charlie is the oldest and fought against the Boers in South Africa. Later he worked as a barman in a mining town where he traded punches with drunken miners. His return to Stroud is both mysterious and unexpected. Here he marries and lives a secluded life as a woodsman.

Uncle Tom was always popular with women and successfully evades them until he finally marries Auntie Minnie. He is a coachman and a gardener and does extraordinary tricks with his eyebrows.

Uncle Ray is depicted as a figure larger than life; a pioneer who helped build the Canadian Pacific Railway. His visits are unpredictable but the children love his boisterous games, tattooed good looks and racy humour. He survives an explosion in the Rockies and is rescued by Aunt Elsie who finally tames him.

How realistic are the accounts of the different uncles' deeds?

Uncle Sid is smaller but no less heroic. He too served in the Boer War. His prowess as a cricketer earns him privileges in the army and admiration from the children. In civilian life his job as a coach driver and reputation as a drinker are at odds. Eventually his drinking earns him a series of suspensions but it is always Sid who is most relieved when his comical and half-hearted suicide attempts come to nothing (p. 183).

This section ends in reflection since Laurie Lee's uncles belong to a bygone era.

James Watson's main body of work consists of novels set around the experiences of young people today.

This section spans a significant period of history. Laurie Lee's uncles have experienced several conflicts. Charlie and Sid witnessed the fighting in South Africa during the Boer War and all five uncles survived the First World War in Europe (p. 169).

To Laurie Lee they are 'legends' who belong to 'another age'. After all, they are horsemen, sons of a coachman. Subsequent wars would not be fought in trenches or on horseback so 'the army released them to a different world' (p. 170).

When Laurie Lee marvels at the adventures of his uncles we see the imagination of a young child at work. There is the description of Uncle Sid hitting yet

FAMILY AND RELATIVES

another six 'his shoulders bursting out of his braces' (p. 179).

In France all five uncles unite against the common enemy, 'riders of hell and apocalypse' (p. 169). In the absence of media and television the children create their own comic book heroes.

GLOSSARY   **Boer War** conflict in South Africa involving British forces (1899–1902)

Identify the characters.

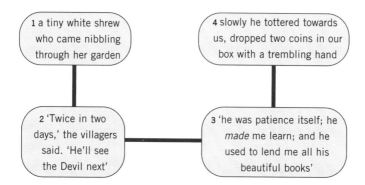

1 a tiny white shrew who came nibbling through her garden

4 slowly he tottered towards us, dropped two coins in our box with a trembling hand

2 'Twice in two days,' the villagers said. 'He'll see the Devil next'

3 'he was patience itself; he *made* me learn; and he used to lend me all his beautiful books'

Identify the person 'to whom' this comment refers.

5 He spread a sheaf of pound notes along the bar and fished a fat gold watch from his pocket

Check your answers on page 77.

 Consider these issues.

a How the portraits of the two grannies help to develop a sense of the village and its past.

b Why the villagers are united against the local man who left to make his fortune.

c The effect of breaking the account to relate the entire story of the author's mother's life.

d The villagers attitude to the Squire and the Big House.

e How life is dictated by nature and the seasons.

f The way childhood illnesses shape the character of the writer.

g How the uncles remind us of the theme of time and change.

CHAPTER **11** – OUTINGS AND FESTIVALS

Colourful celebrations organised by the church or the Squire are focal points in the village calendar. Laurie recalls the festival on Peace Day 1919 at the end of the First World War. Marjorie prepares fancy dress for the children and Laurie Lee appears as a young John Bull. During the procession his costume comes apart and he falls behind but the day ends splendidly with prizes, speeches and photographs in the grounds of the 'Big House'.

In fine weather the family might go blackberry picking or walk to Sheepscombe to visit Uncle Charlie. The children reacquaint themselves with their cousins before the long walk home in the dark.

Choir outings to Gloucester or Bristol become steadily more adventurous. Charabancs replace horse drawn wagons. The village prepares for the faraway Weston-super-Mare. On the day of the outing Mrs Lee is late but eventually the vicar, in pyjamas and overcoat waves the party off. The seaside is a foreign landscape. There is a muddy beach to explore, where Laurie Lee examines a crab, or the pier with its amusements and freak shows. A penny buys a peep at a 'Newgate hanging' (p. 195). On the long journey home the children doze. Laurie Lee dreams of the seaside and mud.

What are our impressions of village life?

In winter the schoolhouse stages the Parochial Church Tea and Annual Entertainment. The Squire's halting speech opens the proceedings followed by jokes and a prayer from the vicar. Among the sketches and comic turns provided by the villagers, Marjorie stars in a short play as Cinderella and Laurie Lee delivers pieces on the violin. The star of the show is a professional singer called Baroness von Hodenburg from Sheepscombe. Slapstick sketches round off the perfect evening but

Laurie Lee and his friends return next morning to gorge on the leftovers.

COMMENT   Major celebrations still revolve around the ageing Squire and his generosity. On these occasions a sense of order and propriety still exists. The Squire's ageing mother closes the Peace Day celebrations with a speech on 'the glory of God, the Empire, us' (p. 187). The vicar takes second place in opening the village's winter entertainments.

Similarly the makeshift fancy dress costumes are a reminder of changes brought about by a rapidly expanding world (p. 187). Charlie Chaplin starred in famous silent movies of that era. There are 'soot-faced savages' and a 'wounded soldier' (p. 187) in the procession too.

How does Laurie Lee convey the day trippers' excitement at the seaside?   Nevertheless it is a close-knit community that is described in this section (see Theme on Village Life). The day trippers to Weston-super-Mare peer out at the comical farming methods beyond Stroud and the valley but look around at each other for the comfort and security they share (p. 193).

CHAPTER 12 – FIRST BITE AT THE APPLE

Around the age of eleven or twelve Laurie Lee begins to take an interest in girls. Jo is a shy girl who Laurie Lee meets on the way home from school. Together they go 'down the bank' (p. 203) to play games of doctors and patients until two cowmen spot them and make fun.

Bet and Rosie who are older and more aware of their influence over the local boys replace Jo (see Characters). They are 'brazen' and 'provocative' (p. 207) and fascinate Laurie Lee and his gang of friends, for whom girls are no longer, simply 'makeshift boys' (p. 206).

GROWING UP

One summer Laurie Lee and Brother Jack help out at the farm at haymaking time. The author stumbles upon Rosie Burdock behind one of the haycocks. She offers him cider to drink and leads him to the bottom of the field. They spend a drowsy afternoon together beneath one of the wagons. It is his first and last encounter with Rosie. He stumbles home in the dark, dazed by the experience and 'was never the same again' (p. 211).

Older now, the author and his friends plan what they term 'the Brith Wood rape' (p. 211), a naive attempt to ambush Lizzy Berkeley on her way home from chapel. She is a plump sixteen-year-old and a devout Christian, known to walk through Brith Wood inscribing religious slogans on the trees.

During the long wait the gang of boys grow uneasy. When Lizzy eventually appears two of the boys bar her way. As she makes her clumsy getaway, after hitting them twice with her bag of crayons, the absurdity of their plan finally dawns on the boys, who never mention it again.

Bill Shepherd, Walt Kerry and the rest of the gang will soon marry. Jo marries a baker from Painswick and Bet emigrates. Rosie Burdock, the author comments, 'married a soldier and I lost her forever' (p. 215).

COMMENT   Midway through this section the author intrudes to remind us of the village's own codes and morals. These 'early sex games' (p. 205) are simply imitations of nature.

Similarly, perhaps to prepare us for the dubious Brith Wood rape story, we are warned that the village may be 'as corrupt as any other community ... as any London Street' (p. 205). Countless crimes flourish in the village (p. 206). However, just as the village 'protected itself' so it punishes the guilty itself too. These sinners are 'given hell, taunted' but not reported. 'There was no tale-bearing then or ringing up 999' (p. 205) (see Theme on Village Life).

In a way, the incident at Brith Wood serves to illustrate this philosophy. An adolescent and misguided idea backfires and the boys are shamed and embarrassed by their actions rather than punished by any outside authority.

In the middle section how is the farm at the height of summer an appropriate **setting** (see Literary Terms) for *In what way is the title to this chapter significant?* Laurie Lee's chance meeting with Rosie? How might descriptions of nature suggest the Garden of Eden in the Bible where Adam is tempted and sins? (p. 209).

Images (see Literary Terms) suggesting danger and excitement add to the tension in this section. Rosie is as 'perilous as quicksand' and the cider jar is 'like an unexploded bomb' (p. 209).

When the writer comments on an 'evening that dilates the memory, even now' (p. 210), what are his feelings about what happened?

Identify the characters.

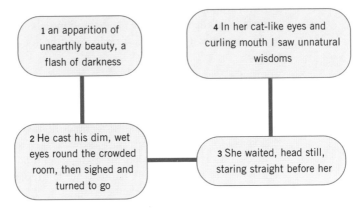

1 an apparition of unearthly beauty, a flash of darkness

4 In her cat-like eyes and curling mouth I saw unnatural wisdoms

2 He cast his dim, wet eyes round the crowded room, then sighed and turned to go

3 She waited, head still, staring straight before her

Identify the person 'to whom' this comment refers.

5 went to sea and won prizes for cooking, then married into the fish-frying business

Check your answers on page 77.

 Consider these issues.

a The way descriptions of fancy dress reiterate character.

b Reminders that the Squire's influence has weakened.

c The closeness of the community.

d The villagers' lack of knowledge of the world beyond the valley.

e The author's use of humour.

f How the author's affection for the community and its resourcefulness is communicated.

CHAPTER **13** – LAST DAYS

By the time Laurie Lee reaches his early teens he has
begun to sense changes to the 'old life' (p. 217) as he
terms it. Motor cars and motorbikes disturb rural peace
and quiet (see Theme on Time and Change). New
people arrive with new ideas. Everything appears the
same but in retrospect major changes to 'a thousand
years' life' (p. 216) are nearly complete.

*What mood is
established at the
start of the final
section?*

The church reflects these changes to the patterns of
village life. Parishioners go obediently to church on
Sunday morning. Afterwards there is a chance to gossip
before Sunday lunch and an afternoon nap. Later, for
Laurie Lee and his fellow choirboys there is a muted
evensong for a 'few solitary worshippers' (p. 220).

The Squire plays his part in spectacular Harvest
Festivals displays. The church is crammed with
admiring villagers and the produce of another year but
when the Squire dies, along with many other of his
generation a way of life dies with him. His great house
is sold off as a 'Home for Invalids' (p. 222) and his
servants find factory jobs.

Meanwhile Laurie Lee's sisters have begun courting
and soon the house is filled with gentlemen callers. On

the day the boiler-works catches fire (p. 224) Marjorie
introduces the family to Maurice. Shortly afterwards
Dorothy meets a scoutmaster named Leslie and Phyllis
falls for a bootmaker called Harold.

Their boyfriends join the family on a picnic but they are
clearly impatient to be rid of the family and have the
sisters to themselves.

The girls themselves are impatient to leave. One night a
heated argument breaks out. In the end the entire
family join in the brawl to prevent one young man
taking their sister from them. It is unclear which sister
he refers to. Laurie Lee remembers the prolonged
goodbyes last thing at night as his sisters take their turn
at the door to see their boyfriends off. Inevitably the
girls are soon engaged and married.

Brother Jack now attends Grammar School; their
mother is old and grows absent-minded.

What is the mood
of the final
section?

The arrival of the wireless brings the outside world even
closer. Laurie Lee is older now and begins to write
poems. He is less content with the world around him
and restless to fulfil his own ambition.

COMMENT

The theme of change is dealt with more directly now
(see Theme on Time and Change). What are the
writer's feelings at the fragmentation of family and
community? To what extent is his own restlessness a
part of this process? Is he too drawn by these 'new
excitements'?

Laurie Lee is keen to point out how important a role
the church plays in rural life. Harvest Festival is a time
of abundance and renewal. However, look more closely
at changes of mood in the description of a typical
Sunday (p. 220); why might the writer choose to
describe the church in such contrasting ways; thriving
in the morning, sombre and quiet by evening?

Why are the
'young men' (p.
225) who visit, so
wary of Laurie
Lee's mother?

On the picnic that the writer describes, we are reminded of his mother's warm but chaotic hospitality as she organises the reluctant boyfriends. She is 'determined to make the thing go' (p. 227).

In the final section Laurie Lee appears to be explaining what led him to a career as a writer. What does he mean when he says 'voices elected me of all men living and called me to deliver the world' (pp. 230–1)? In the last paragraph he sits alone, unhurried by time, composing poems about what he sees. Why is he so anxious to record what he has experienced?

GLOSSARY   ***Sons and Lovers*** novel by D.H. Lawrence which caused sensation on publication

TEST YOURSELF (CHAPTER 13)

 Identify the characters.

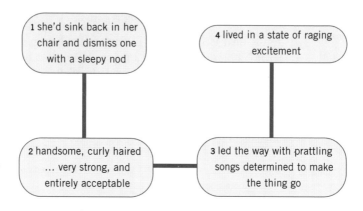

1 she'd sink back in her chair and dismiss one with a sleepy nod

4 lived in a state of raging excitement

2 handsome, curly haired ... very strong, and entirely acceptable

3 led the way with prattling songs determined to make the thing go

Identify the person 'to whom' this comment refers.

6 had strokes and seizures, faced by speeds beyond comprehension

Check your answers on page 77.

 Consider these issues.

a Different symptoms of the dramatic changes reaching the valley.

b The role the church had played in the community.

c The changes that follow the death of the Squire.

d The effects on the family as the girls begin courting.

e Changes in the relationship between the village and the outside world.

f The author's feelings in relation to the place of his childhood, and himself.

PART THREE

COMMENTARY

THEMES

GROWING UP

A romantic view of childhood

Laurie Lee once wrote that his purpose in looking back over his childhood was to 'praise' the life he had enjoyed as a youth. A modern reader can take pleasure from the more romanticised accounts of a rural upbringing. When Laurie Lee describes summer as a child it is idyllic and endless. The author pictures himself lying on a sunny bank, chewing grass and then lists the sounds and sensations of a perfect summer's afternoon (p. 151). 'Village Winter' is given a similar treatment with the descriptions of Christmas card **images** (see Literary Terms): deep snow, skating on the frozen pond and carol-singing at the remote Joseph's farm.

A deprived childhood

The harshness of his childhood is unmistakable too. The Lee family are in a precarious state when the story begins. Mrs Lee is a single parent with a family of eight children. The cottage they rent is ramshackle and damp; mushrooms grow from the ceiling. They are poor and their muddle-headed mother struggles to manage what little money they have. Allowing for exaggeration, the children are reared on a meagre diet of porridge, lentil stew, cabbage and bread. Laurie Lee's classmates at the village school can only aspire to the manual work that awaits them in the surrounding fields, for which they are being prepared. It is a narrow and stifling upbringing. The Lees' standard of living would rival anything in the towns and cities of the era.

A sense of attachment

Perhaps the writer's success in recreating his childhood for us is due to the rigid limits his world imposed upon him. Look at the way he presents life at the village

*Would we recall
our childhood with
the same clarity?*
school. It has little to offer and the writer is often
critical and unsentimental. However, strong emotions
add colour and life to a section that remains most
memorable. A toddler's world and that of a teenager are
summoned up with remarkable intensity.

Through television and the media, travel and education,
children today enjoy a wealth of experience. Laurie
Lee's childhood was stifling by comparison but rich in
the sense of attachment he felt for family, community,
time and place.

TIME AND CHANGE

The changes that the author must have witnessed in his
lifetime could hardly be more dramatic. For this reason
his urge to preserve the world of his upbringing and to
point out change, is insistent in the story.

*Does this new
freedom and
mobility bring
change for the
better?*
Horses governed the shape of the land and the pace of
life at the turn of the century. 'His eight miles an hour
was … the size of our world' (p. 216) comments Laurie
Lee. During the course of the story wagon trips to
Gloucester are replaced by breathless charabanc outings
to faraway Weston-super-Mare.

Laurie Lee's grandfather's inn, The Plough, survived on
the passing trade of carters. A coachman himself, we
can only imagine what John Light's reaction would
have been to see narrow lanes suddenly cluttered with
motorbikes and cars.

Slad lies up the valley from the railways and canals
brought by the Industrial Revolution. It is the 1920s
and factories may be in decline, but each morning
Laurie Lee's sisters are still a part of the hectic traffic in
the lane heading for the shops and mills of Stroud. A
narrow life offered by the Squire and menial jobs on the
land or about the estate offer little attraction for the
girls. Dorothy's wages earned as a clerk at a 'decayed

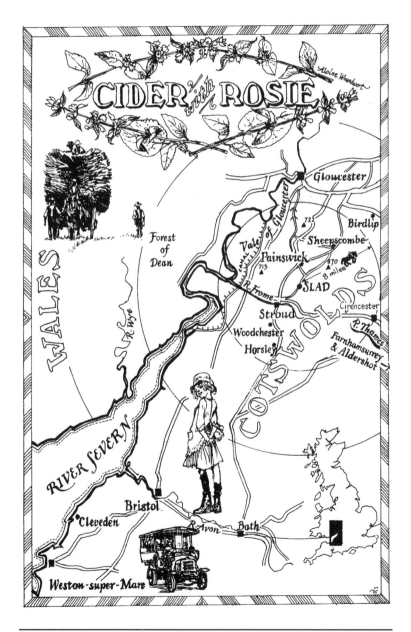

cloth mill', presumably pay for the fashions displayed at the milliners where Marjorie works, or footwear from 'Boots and Shoes', Phyllis's employer.

What aspects of life 'below stars' (p. 116) does their mother recall so fondly?

Laurie Lee's mother romanticising about her days as a maid to the gentry, and Granny Trill and Granny Wallon with their strict codes and elaborate dress remind us of an ordered and bygone era. The Squire makes frequent appearances but he is old and frail and when he dies his home is auctioned off as a home for invalids. In the final section, as the older folk 'who thee'd and thou'd' (p. 222) begin to disappear, a way of life, a set of values, disappear with them.

Isolated stories that the narrator selects for us are suddenly significant when we realise that we are watching something that might never be repeated.

With reference to the Ice Age and the valley's origins the writer places events against a larger time frame. In the present, new ways threaten traditions shaped by generations of local people. As Laurie Lee puts it, 'that continuous contact has at last been broken, the deeper coves sealed off forever' (p. 105).

As a teenager Laurie Lee became impatient to move on, himself, but the story remains as a faithful record of village life at the start of the century, before it was allowed to 'break, dissolve and scatter' (p. 217).

VILLAGE LIFE

From the outset the village and its portrayal is something of a contradiction. It is restricting and insular and yet it is also the entire world to its inhabitants, for whom Gloucester was 'once a foreign city' (p. 217). Its limitations are the straitjackets that force the author to leave in search of adventure as a teenager, yet ironically with its character and history the village has already given up a wealth of experience; the very subject of the writer's work.

Once the infant Laurie Lee has come to terms with his immediate surroundings in the opening chapter, his attentions turn to the village as a whole. At first he is frightened and bewildered by what he sees but it is here that he will receive its unique form of instruction.

The description that opens the chapter 'Village School' is hardly promising; a damp gully with a scattering of houses 'a church, a chapel, a vicarage, ... a pub' (p. 42). Later we see that the village strength arises from its ability to provide for itself, from its closeness and resourcefulness. In the absence of ready-made entertainment there are celebrations, feasts, festivals, outings and gatherings, home-made entertainment that make Laurie Lee's childhood seem an enviable one.

In winter the author and his friends have ice skating on Jones's pond to occupy their time. At Christmas time rival troops of carol singers compete for the village's hospitality. In summer, games like Fox and Hounds take in the village and the surrounding woods and fields. The narrow curriculum of the school cannot compete. No wonder the noises of life outside the classroom 'tugged and pulled at our active wishes till we could have done Miss B a murder' (p. 50).

The village's foundations go deep, we are reminded, with tales and traditions that help shape the character of the young writer. Although in its final stages of decline the hierarchy from Church or Squire to peasant has ordered the lives of generations and some sense of this harmony, or loss of it, is mourned in the author's portrayal of village life.

How does village life compare with life in the city according to the author? (p. 205)

The closeness of such a community has advantages and disadvantages. It is a place where secrets are quickly discovered. Laurie Lee's early experiments with girls are

quickly observed and checked. The village seems cut off
from written laws of the town, and local custom or
opinion is the natural authority. Witness the brutal
justice that a local man receives on his homecoming in
the section 'Public Death, Private Murder'. In direct
contrast Joe and Hannah Brown are forced to leave the
village for the workhouse and perish there. Characters
arrange themselves within the many stories according to
their loyalty to village life.

World events and local events are often contrasted. The
young writer learns of current affairs through their
impact on his immediate surroundings. Beyond the
valley these events often seem remote or insignificant.
As the young Laurie Lee comments, the end of the war
is virtually undetectable, 'food tasted the same, pump
water was as cold' (p. 25).

STRUCTURE

The structure of Laurie Lee's **autobiography** (see
Literary Terms) does not follow a strict or predictable
pattern. The reader is introduced to the author as a
three year old when he is unrolled, screaming, from a
Union Jack in the first chapter. By the end of chapter 3
the village school has transformed the infant into a
teenager with little left to learn, who roams the
playground with his gang, 'just a punch here and there

Does this lack of   to show our authority' (p. 58). The chapter entitled
order spoil our   'Sick Boy' retraces earlier memories when the author
enjoyment of the   was eighteen months old. By this time we are happy for
story?   the writer to include a diversity of character and
incident as part of a sequence that is not chronological
at all.

Careful   An impression of the writer's early life is built around
selection   memorable episodes. Laurie Lee described this

method like 'summer's lightning', choosing to begin with those moments where 'the light sparkled brightest'. Sometimes chapters are devoted to individuals, like his mother or uncles, or similar ideas grouped together. Either way, careful selection makes the text more unexpected and revealing. Rather like the household he describes on page 13, the story itself is 'shaken many times, like a snow-storm toy', but the details the writer settles on are the most memorable ones.

Economy   To avoid missing things out some chapters follow a structure of their own that enables the writer a greater freedom in the details he can include. The description of a single day at school is actually everyday of the author's school career in the sense that it is crammed with every possible experience. The description of a typical Sunday in the final chapter goes much further. It is about the Sunday routine but manages to chart the churches decline and define the changing relationship of church to its community.

CHARACTERS

LAURIE LEE   Writing about Laurie Lee in *Cider with Rosie* is not as simple as it might appear. The author as a three-year-old is the focus of the opening section because of the limitations of his world, but gradually, as he gains experience it is as if a camera turns away from the writer towards the new experiences around him. So instead of a self-portrait, the story begins to look outward and the writer becomes 'a presence, a listening shadow' (see Laurie Lee's *I Can't Stay Long*, 1975).

In the section entitled 'Village School' for instance, the disgruntled infant who would prefer to stay at home is soon able to cope and we begin to lose sight of him amid all the other activities of the playground and classroom.

A further complication arises here, when the older author appears with his more worldly opinions on childhood and the education he received.

Early years

As a member of a large family the young Laurie Lee seems naturally boisterous, refusing to go to school, or annoyed that his eyes are stuck together, "'who did it?' I yelled' (p. 17). He is jealous of his mother's affections and protective too, curious to sample newly discovered delights, gorging himself on garden vegetables.

Dark corners of the house and stories from the older girls feed his imagination. He learns about death when he discovers dead animals in the garden. His fascination emerges through the descriptions; 'bird's gaping bones … silent-roaring city of a cat's grub-captured carcass' (p. 14). The more sinister tales from local folklore absorb him later. The same imagination glorifies the young Laurie Lee as a future King who will provide Princes for his beautiful sisters.

Imaginative
Outgoing
Loyal
Inquisitive

The writer's mother and sisters are prominent in his upbringing. He admires them all and enjoys the closeness of their crowded household.

School life and
after

At school Laurie Lee describes himself as unremarkable although this may be in comparison to high-flying Jack, his older and more academic brother. Younger brother Tony can be cheeky; Laurie Lee is the 'drowsy middleman' (p. 53). We can picture 'Loll' as an infant, sometimes outspoken, lazing in the arms of the beautiful harp-playing assistant teacher 'leaning her bosom against our faces and guiding our wandering fingers' (p. 44).

Natural curiosity runs contrary to authority now when Laurie Lee decides to hit Vera with a beech stick to see its effect on her 'springy hair' (p. 147). The two girls he shares a table with, Poppy and Jo, irritate him. Their 'female self possession' makes him 'shout angrily at them' (p. 45).

Laurie lee describes his younger self as 'idle' and 'content to slop about' (p. 48). He clearly enjoyed school even if he is dismissive of his successes. The fake essay on otters wins praise from Miss Wardley although he'd 'never seen an otter or even gone to look for one' (p. 53).

Increasingly the author uses 'we' or 'our' and describes groups he belongs to rather than distinguishing himself; the choir, his family, the village gang.

Only illness distinguishes the young Laurie Lee and makes him feel special. He claims to have survived his own precarious childhood almost at the expense of his sister Frances who died aged four. In the section 'Sick Boy' he describes these fevers, the voices he hears and the peculiar visions and dreams. Perhaps these fuel an already vivid imagination. At times he enjoys the renewed affections and attentions sickness brings.

Look again at the way the writer uses language to describe a fever.

Adolescence and beyond

Much of Laurie Lee's teenage years are described in terms of the gang he spends time with, 'scuffling, fighting, aimless and dangerous, confused by our strength and boredom' (p. 211). Now girls are strange and interesting. Jo, his infant classmate, is the silent accomplice in his experimental games. Bet and Rosie, the older girls, baffle him.

Finally the author seems more solitary. He is intrigued by the world beyond the valley. He now writes poetry and is a more self-conscious figure, 'I groaned from solitude, blushed when I stumbled' (p. 231).

MOTHER

Laurie Lee reserves one chapter to sketch in his mother's past life and character, but from the start of the story she is as prominent a figure as the author is.

First impressions

We first meet her on the day of their arrival. She is as energetic as the younger girls are but even with the burden of house moving she enjoys the distraction of filling pots and jugs with flowers from the garden. At the end of the first section she 'disappears' to visit their father, presumably in an attempt to patch up their broken marriage. Midway through the chapter the stranger who appears in the kitchen, a deserter, is given porridge and sympathy. She sleeps, 'like a happy child' (p. 27), exhausted from housework at the start of the next section. By the end of the chapter we see her battling against the elements to repel the floods. Already she is a picture of self-sacrifice. The odds are against her but she is devoted to her family.

Past life

Loyal
Disorganised
Self-sacrificing
Creative
Generous

Her own youth is consistent with this pattern. She is bright and receptive at school but sacrifices her education at thirteen to nurse her sick mother. As a maid to the gentry she learns to tend to others' needs and later comes to the aid of her father as a barmaid at the inn he acquires in Sheepscombe. We can imagine how isolated a time this must have seemed to a young woman. She remains faithful to her father until an ad in the paper for a housekeeper leads her to find her husband and Laurie Lee's father.

Compassion towards others

It is worth registering her opinions and asides to the children. She understandS the plight of the solitary Miss Flynn who later drowns herself (p. 100), and is a sympathetic ear and agony aunt for old Mrs Davies and her sick husband (p. 107) – 'It was like this Mrs Lee'. She reminds the children of the need to be tolerant of their elderly neighbour Granny Trill – '"Don't mock," said our mother, "the poor, poor soul – alone by herself all day"' (p. 89).

Faithful wife and mother

As proof of her fidelity Laurie Lee's mother raises both her husband's and her own children single-handedly and waits thirty-five years for the 'praise' she deserves but never gets. Her frustrations manifest themselves in different ways. There are irrational outbursts at her predicament and there are other moments when she reminisces about the early years of their marriage. Weaving silk and bits of jewellery she indulges in thoughts of the happiest years of her life.

Her beauty is often associated with her efforts to care for others. As she encourages Laurie Lee in his attempts at the violin he comments 'old and tired though she was, her eyes were a girl's, and it was for looks such as these that I played' (p. 71). We are told that she always eats standing up and her constant efforts to keep the fire alive come to symbolise her continual effort to care (p. 72).

FATHER
Charming
Respectable
Educated
Remote
Selfish
Cowardly

Reg Lee's photograph surveys the family from its place on the wall of the living room but his expression is haughty and cold and Laurie Lee doesn't attempt to disguise his lack of feeling for the man. Pictured like a 'scandalised god' (p. 67), he is a distant figure. As a child Laurie Lee even confuses him with the Kaiser.

What do we learn about the early years of their marriage?

The author traces his father's past in a cold, historical way. He was the son of a soldier but preferred the job of a greengrocer's assistant to a career in the navy. He is left with five children from his first marriage. When his first wife dies he advertises for a housekeeper. Laurie Lee's mother answers the advertisement and is instantly attracted to him.

Mr Lee is depicted as a charming, well-mannered man but without substance. Throughout, his portrayal is

coloured by the author's opinion of him. As a young
man, Reg Lee is a fashionable figure, a 'dandy' (p. 60).
In contrast to the heroic uncles he survives a 'clerk-stool
war' (p. 61) as a civil servant. His visits to the family
home are infrequent and 'fugitive' (p. 60). Instead he
sends a meagre few pounds as housekeeping. Even in
the early days of their marriage he is preoccupied with
his books not his children.

In the end his narrow respectability and gentility are
entirely out of keeping with the family he leaves
behind. He is portrayed as undeserving of his wife's
faith and devotion. His eventual death by 'cranking his
car in a Morden suburb' (p. 135) is as remote as he was
himself.

MARJORIE

Kind

Gentle

Unselfish

Motherly

Beautiful

Marjorie is the oldest of Laurie Lee's half-sisters.
Consequently she takes a share in the running of the
household, particularly on occasions when Laurie's
mother goes away (p. 20). Aged fourteen, she is a tall
pretty girl with long blond hair. Whenever crises arise
she is a calming influence, ready to reassure. Laurie Lee
admires her but comments that Marjorie was
unconscious of her charm and beauty.

Does Laurie Lee

object to an

upbringing

surrounded by

females?

Aged sixteen she is at her most stunning, (p. 185), and
for the Peace Day Parade she has prepared the
children's' costumes herself. She is talented at making
clothes and works for a milliner in the town. During
the celebrations she makes a breathtaking appearance as
Queen Elizabeth but it is typical of her modest beauty
and gentle nature that she should play the part of
Cinderella at the village entertainments (p. 200). When
she marries it is to Maurice a barge builder and a choice
entirely approved of by the family.

DOROTHY

If Marjorie is described as a 'steady flame', by contrast
Dorothy is the firework (p. 62). She is less prominent
in the story than Marjorie but contributes with her taste

Adventurous
Chatty
Lively
Outgoing

for relaying gossip to Marjorie's eager ears. Early in the story she appears chatty and giggly but is clearly more adventurous than the others. It is her suggestion to go out and view the drunken celebrations one evening when news of the peace reaches the village. Marjorie is alarmed when fights break out outside the local pub whereas Dorothy is 'shocked and delighted' (p. 23). Perhaps we associate her with new ways and new ideas – working as she does in one of the town's cloth factories. She is a lively, interesting character with a gentle side too. She is kind and protective towards her half-brothers. Dealing with the attentions of local boys she shows confidence and composure.

Later in fancy dress she appears as 'Night' in a spectacular spangled black costume. She eventually falls for her opposite, Leslie, who is a shy scoutmaster, we are told, 'until he met her' (p. 225).

Phyllis
The odd one out
Generous
Quiet

Phyllis is the youngest of the three and the solitary one. She amuses herself while Marjorie and Dorothy are absorbed by the latest news. Laurie Lee recalls her singing to them. Her sombre hymns would send them to sleep. She is grave and sensible, a little old fashioned but above all generous, 'quick to admire and slow to complain' (p. 62).

In her teens she works at a shoe shop in Stroud and meets and marries a bootmaker called Harold who entertains the family with his piano playing.

Frances

Laurie Lee remembers Frances as a watchful four-year-old beside his cot. We are not told of the cause of her death, only that it might have been avoided and that in some peculiar way she transmitted to Laurie Lee the strength to survive the illnesses that threatened his life in childhood (p. 157). Laurie Lee's mother we are told would regularly cry at the thought of the death of her four-year-old daughter.

BROTHERS

Jack Elder brother Jack is Laurie Lee's true brother, bedfellow and companion. The two enjoy each other's company but when disagreements do occur both resort to a comical game of whistling and singing to annoy the other (p. 65). Laurie Lee joins the infant class when Jack has clearly outgrown it. He is the studious member of the family, 'the accepted genius' and is often absorbed in his studies detached from the others. The writer describes him demanding the attentions of

Why does the author describe Jack as an 'Infant Freak'? (p. 47) teachers or clearing the kitchen table at home to complete homework by candlelight. By the final chapter Jack attends the grammar school. Perhaps the author admires his academic brother. Nevertheless they share a close relationship. Jack is lively and fun too. He gobbles his food and is nicknamed 'the slider' at mealtimes. On Peace Day he refuses to dress up but settles on a Robin Hood costume in the end.

Tony Younger brother Tony's birth coincides with a particularly serious illness when Laurie Lee was only eighteen months old. When Laurie Lee is three he and Tony become rivals for a place in their mother's bed. At the local school Tony is the most difficult of the three, 'impervious either to learning or authority' (p. 53). At home he is the odd one out. The author mentions his talent for drawing and his bravery, the countless beads he swallowed and finally his excellent singing voice. Rather like Phyllis, Tony remains in the background, 'the tiny hermit no one quite understood' (p. 63).

Reggie Laurie Lee had two half-brothers from his father's previous marriage. Reggie is the oldest but lives elsewhere with his grandmother.

Harold Harold is the other half-brother and misses his father. In his teens he is up at six o'clock in time for work at a factory lathe. He enjoys his job but we are told that he is often 'secretive' and 'unhappy' (p. 63). He appears a solitary character although sparse references make his portrait less defined.

THE UNCLES

Uncle Charlie   Uncle Charlie boasts the achievement of having taken part in both the Boer War and the First World War. When the Boer War ended he worked as a barman in a South African mining town. In his broad Gloucestershire accent he recounts tales of his brawls and adventures, for the children.

Later he settles down with a local girl, Fanny Causon. He enjoys work as a forester but is poorly paid.

Uncle Tom   Uncle Tom has one particularly memorable feature. Comically the children attribute his success with women to the tricks he can perform with his eyebrows. He is fashionable and a ladies' man. He manages to resist their attentions but eventually succumbs and marries Auntie Minnie.

Uncle Ray

If we are to trust the author's account, Uncle Ray almost single-handedly built the Canadian Transcontinental Railway. He is an unpredictable hero, rugged, tanned, tattooed and handsome. He is popular with the children enjoying rough and tumble games, but he is childish in his own way, victim to his wild impulses. The author describes Uncle Ray in a colourful and affectionate way. He is a unique and 'exotic' figure; 'a gift of the devil to us, a monstrous toy, a good natured freak' (p. 176). As well as his striking appearance he has a stock of ready one-liners and leaves the children in fits of giggles. 'See you all in the oven. Scrub yer elbows ... So long' (p. 176). Visits are punctuated by drinking bouts and awkward scrapes with local girls. Eventually he settles down with Auntie Elsie, a schoolteacher, after a near fatal accident in Canada on the railways.

Uncle Sid	Uncle Sid was a soldier too. During the Boer War in South Africa his greatest achievements were on the cricket field. After the wars he became a bus driver. He is less heroic or handsome than Uncle Ray but no less willing to deal out justice in a single punch to the scoundrel and wife-beater they encounter on a charabanc outing. Drink is his downfall and after ignoring countless warnings from the bus company he stages a series of bungled suicide attempts as a plea for attention. Laurie Lee's mother becomes accustomed to his wife, Aunt Alice's hysteria when Uncle Sid disappears each time.
Uncle George	Uncle George is the only relative who does not inspire the children's admiration. He is Reg Lee's brother and dismissed as a 'rogue' who sold newspapers.
John Light	John Light is their mother's father; he was a coachman who was apparently famed for his handsome legs. He passes on his skill as a horseman to his sons. Later he is pictured as the easy-going landlord of 'The Plough' in Sheepscombe, enjoying a drink and singing for the customers while his daughter is left to deal with rowdy drunks.

GRANNIES

Granny Wallon	Tiny and shrew-like, Granny Wallon is to be found hunting the garden for ingredients to make her potent wines with. So resourceful is she that the author suggests she might make a 'drink out of a box of old matches' (p. 80). Granny Wallon is a frail creature seen 'nibbling' around her garden, 'or sat sucking bread in the sun.' (p. 78) She is solitary but 'self contained'. From time to time she appears at the kitchen window, 'squeaking with gossip,' and is a regular visitor with jugs of her potent wine. Her children have grown up and departed long ago and her feud with 'Er-Up-Atop'

occupies her time. She outlives her rival but causes a commotion at the funeral of Granny Trill, outraged at the thought of her having the last word (p. 93).

Granny Trill   Constantly chewing, obeying a routine independent of others Granny Trill is described as having an 'original sense of time' (p. 82). She plots the future with the aid of her almanac but she is as old as the beech tree planted in the garden by her father. Ironically, she shares her sense of propriety and manners with Granny Wallon downstairs but the mention of her name sends her into fits of rage. She fondly remembers her childhood; the beautiful daughter of a woodcutter, taken in by the Squire at fifteen when her father was killed by a falling tree. Granny Trill is both frugal and severe. She is outraged when Marjorie, Dorothy and Phyllis dress up to entertain her, and outspoken in her criticism of them later. 'Humble gels got to remember their stations'. (p. 91). When she slips and breaks her hip she accepts death with dignified resignation.

THE SQUIRE

Old
Frail
Generous

The Squire is an important figure in the story, a survivor of the village's semi-feudal past. He presides over major functions, he appears at the school, he praises and rewards, and his house and gardens are a source of employment. The village benefits from his generosity and fatherly hospitality but he is old and frail. He is portrayed affectionately and we remember carefully-selected details; the trembling hand that scratches a name in the carol singers book, (p. 144), the emotional but incoherent speech at the village Entertainment, appropriately enough on the theme of time (p. 198).

On Peace Day, his mother recalls the days of the glorious British Empire in her speech (p. 187). In church the Squire's place is reserved next to the Lords of the Manor. The writer comically compares God to him; 'a kind of Squire-archical rent-collector' (p. 219).

His eventual death is described as a benevolent supporting hand withdrawn, and there is a certain unease in the writer's voice when the Squire's house becomes a home for invalids, a sign that the natural order within the village has finally broken down.

OTHER CHARACTERS

Cabbage-Stump Charlie	Among the villagers, Cabbage-Stump Charlie is a notorious fighter. His name arises from the cabbage-stalk he uses to club his unfortunate victims.
Albert the Devil	Villagers leave money or food on their garden walls rather than face Albert the Devil. He is deaf, mute and a beggar. Locals fear his alarming appearance and unnerving stare.
Percy-from-Painswick	Percy is a harmless tramp from Painswick. He entertains the children and taunts girls in particular with his outrageous comments.
Prospect Smiler	Prospect Smiler is a local farmer whose face is paralysed into a permanent grin. His smiling face and alarming insults would unnerve newcomers to the village.
Willy the Fish	On Fridays, Willy sells fish door-to-door in the village. He smells which accounts for the loss of his girlfriend.
Mr Jolly	Mr Jolly is to blame for Laurie Lee's mother's interest in books and fine things. He was the schoolmaster from Quedgeley who did his utmost to develop her potential as a student until she abandoned her education to tend her sick mother. He was an elderly but talented teacher.
Mr and Mrs Davies	The elderly Davies couple live near the village shop. Mr Davies refuses any operation to cure his pneumonia.

Old and withered in his freezing bedroom Mr Davies's frail figure is lodged in the author's memory.

Joseph and Hannah Brown

The Browns are a happy self-contained couple but when they become too old to care for themselves they are banished to separate wings of the Workhouse. Content to live out their natural lives in the valley, their story serves to remind us of unnatural laws imposed by the world outside (see Theme on Time and Change).

Miss Flynn

Miss Flynn is a solitary and reclusive character who lives across the valley. She is a pale, beautiful but tormented figure who is later found drowned in the local pond.

Fred Bates

Fred Bates delivers the milk. He wins temporary fame when he discovers the body of Miss Flynn in the nearby pond. When he witnesses a man crushed by a wagon in Stroud the very next day, villagers are suddenly wary of him.

Vincent

Returning from New Zealand having made his fortune farming there, Vincent boasts of his triumphs at the local inn. He goads the locals for their lack of adventure but is later discovered in a ditch, robbed of his valuables, kicked and beaten to death.

Miss B

She teaches the junior schoolchildren who nickname her 'Crabby' for her manner and appearance. She makes a striking portrait. She has 'lank' hair, a 'sour' complexion, and resembles a turkey. She terrorises the children, barking orders and pouncing on miscreants, but her bark is proved to be worse than her bite when Spadge Hopkins challenges her authority.

Miss Wardley

The more tolerant Miss Wardley from Birmingham replaces 'Crabby B'. She establishes a firmer authority, is direct but realistic. Her patience earns her Laurie Lee's respect and he remembers her jewellery in particular.

Spadge Hopkins	Large for his age Spadge Hopkins resembles a 'bullock in ballet shoes' (p. 50), penned up behind his tiny school desk. Bored with school, he carves his name in the desk with a penknife and impresses his classmates when he rebels against Miss B's unbending authority.
Walt Kerry	Walt Kerry is the school bully who demands the answers to sums from Laurie Lee. As a teenager he is a member of the 'gang'. He later becomes a sailor and marries 'into the fish-frying business' (p. 215).
Poppy and Jo	Poppy and Jo share Laurie Lee's table in the infants. On Peace Day Poppy Green dresses as an Angel and Laurie Lee encourages her to fly by pushing her off the mantelpiece. Jo later becomes a girlfriend, briefly.
Bill Shepherd and 'Boney'	Both number among the aimless gang that Laurie Lee belongs to in his teens. In the choir Boney distinguishes himself by singing flat. He marries an energetic farm-widow. Bill Shepherd is instrumental in planning the Brithwood Rape (p. 212) but is later 'trapped' by a girl who marries him for his post office book.
Betty Gleed	As a teenager Bet is an intimidating figure. The author describes her as 'brazen ... blonde' and as an illustration tells us, 'For a wine gum she would have stripped in church' (p. 207).
Rosie Burdock	Rosie is mysterious, provocative and sly. The author stumbles upon her in his teens, concealed behind the hayrick and she is more a presence than a character. Exciting, dangerous, sensuous, she resembles a mood and an experience. After their memorable afternoon under the hay wagon she disappears 'for good' almost without the author realising, leaving him to make his own way home alone.

Cider with Rosie encompasses more than simply a child's life from age three to adolescence. It is far more ambitious. Other stories, other lives and other times fascinate the writer. Laurie Lee later commented 'my own story would keep, whereas the story of the village would not'. With so much to cram into the pages of his book the writer must employ tremendous economy of style. Read an early section like 'First Names' to appreciate the volume of character anecdote that forms a backdrop to the writer's early life.

Vivid impressions

Often, when recalling a particular occasion the writer brings many other moments to bear on the description. However, instead of getting a general or typical account the result can be far more vivid and wide-ranging. This sort of compression works wonderfully in the school section, and when Laurie Lee describes evenings in the kitchens at home he manages to capture the essence of his home life and a large section of his childhood.

IMAGERY

Language that is rich in **imagery** (see Literary Terms) allows the writer to give clearer pictures for his reader as well as suggesting a whole range of other sensations. Images are drawn from Laurie Lee's experience but are often effective because of their simplicity. It is easy to picture the Grannies in the wainscot with their 'sickle-bent bodies' or the site of their cottage which 'bore into the side of the bank like a rusty expended shell' (p. 78). Even places that may be unfamiliar are conjured up with the same economy. Distant Painswick on the other side of the valley appears to Laurie Lee like 'the skeleton of a foundered mammoth' by day, by night 'a starfish of light' (p. 189).

HUMOUR

Humour arises in the story in many different ways:
- In descriptions of people and their behaviour; Uncle Ray when he is drunk (p. 177) or the eventual discovery of yet another of Uncle Sid's suicide attempts (p. 183).
- In the knowing voice of the author looking back on events.
- In lively dialogue using local dialects; Granny Trill's outburst when compared to her enemy Granny Wallon: 'Er down there! I got more than 'er! Er's bald as a tater root!' (p. 83).

A CHILD'S CHANGING PERSPECTIVE

What are the feelings experienced by the author as a three-year-old boy in the opening passages of the story?

The **narrative** (see Literary Terms) in the opening chapter depicts the world as an infant would see it. The author selects and describes detail in fresh and unexpected ways (see Sample Essay Plan).

As the young Laurie Lee grows so the writer's choice of language must reflect his widening experience and curiosity.

Look for examples of where the writer's choice of words clearly reflects a child's understanding of events.

Part four

Study skills

How to use quotations

One of the secrets of success in writing essays is the way you use quotations. There are five basic principles:

- Put inverted commas at the beginning and end of the quotation
- Write the quotation exactly as it appears in the original
- Do not use a quotation that repeats what you have just written
- Use the quotation so that it fits into your sentence
- Keep the quotation as short as possible

Quotations should be used to develop the line of thought in your essays.

Your comment should not duplicate what is in your quotation. For example:

Laurie Lee and his classmates were afraid of their new teacher, 'We were all afraid of the gobbling Miss B' (p. 49)

Far more effective is to write:

Like his classmates Laurie Lee soon learns to be 'afraid of the gobbling Miss B'.

However, the most sophisticated way of using the writer's words is to embed them into your sentence:

For the young author violence and death are 'absorbing' and accepted with 'a frank and unfearful attitude' (p. 105).

When you use quotations in this way, you are demonstrating the ability to use text as evidence to support your ideas - not simply including words from the original to prove you have read it.

Everyone writes differently. Work through the suggestions given here and adapt the advice to suit your own style and interests. This will improve your essay-writing skills and allow your personal voice to emerge.

The following points indicate in ascending order the skills of essay writing:

- Picking out one or two facts about the story and adding the odd detail
- Writing about the text by retelling the story
- Retelling the story and adding a quotation here and there
- Organising an answer which explains what is happening in the text and giving quotations to support what you write

....

- Writing in such a way as to show that you have thought about the intentions of the writer of the text and that you understand the techniques used
- Writing at some length, giving your viewpoint on the text and commenting by picking out details to support your views
- Looking at the text as a work of art, demonstrating clear critical judgement and explaining to the reader of your essay how the enjoyment of the text is assisted by literary devices, linguistic effects and psychological insights; showing how the text relates to the time when it was written

The dotted line above represents the division between lower and higher level grades. Higher-level performance begins when you start to consider your response as a reader of the text. The highest level is reached when you offer an enthusiastic personal response and show how this piece of literature is a product of its time.

Coursework essay

Set aside an hour or so at the start of your work to plan what you have to do.

- List all the points you feel are needed to cover the task. Collect page references of information and quotations that will support what you have to say. A helpful tool is the highlighter pen: this saves painstaking copying and enables you to target precisely what you want to use.
- Focus on what you consider to be the main points of the essay. Try to sum up your argument in a single sentence, which could be the closing sentence of your essay. Depending on the essay title, it could be a statement about a character: despite her erratic nature, Mrs Lee succeeds in giving her children a stable and loving home life; an opinion about setting: the world of the villagers both isolated and self sufficient; or a judgement on a theme: a gallery of characters from the past helps to remind us of a way of life that has disappeared.
- Make a short essay plan. Use the first paragraph to introduce the argument you wish to make. In the following paragraphs develop this argument with details, examples and other possible points of view. Sum up your argument in the last paragraph. Check you have answered the question.
- Write the essay, remembering all the time the central point you are making.
- On completion, go back over what you have written to eliminate careless errors and improve expression. Read it aloud to yourself, or, if you are feeling more confident, to a relative or friend.

If you can, try to type your essay, using a word processor. This will allow you to correct and improve your writing without spoiling its appearance.

Examination essay

The essay written in an examination often carries more marks than the coursework essay even though it is written under considerable time pressure.

In the revision period build up notes on various aspects of the text you are using. Fortunately, in acquiring this set of York Notes on *Cider with Rosie*, you have made a prudent beginning! York Notes are set out to give you vital information and help you to construct your personal overview of the text.

Make notes with appropriate quotations about the key issues of the set text. Go into the examination knowing your text and having a clear set of opinions about it.

In most English Literature examinations you can take in copies of your set books. This in an enormous advantage although it may lull you into a false sense of security. Beware! There is simply not enough time in an examination to read the book from scratch.

In the examination

- Read the question paper carefully and remind yourself what you have to do.
- Look at the questions on your set texts to select the one that most interests you and mentally work out the points you wish to stress.
- Remind yourself of the time available and how you are going to use it.
- Briefly map out a short plan in note form that will keep your writing on track and illustrate the key argument you want to make.
- Then set about writing it.
- When you have finished, check through to eliminate errors.

To summarise, these are the keys to success:

- **Know the text**
- **Have a clear understanding of and opinions on the storyline, characters, setting, themes and writer's concerns**
- **Select the right material**
- **Plan and write a clear response, continually bearing the question in mind**

SAMPLE ESSAY PLAN

A typical essay question on *Cider with Rosie* is followed by a sample essay plan in note form. You will need to look back through the text to find quotations to support your points. Think about your own ideas – the sample answer is only a suggestion and you may wish to ignore it and produce your own, but it is always a good idea to plan out your thoughts first – it will save you time and help you to organise your ideas. Remember – try to answer the question!

How does the writer succeed in recreating events in the story from the changing perspective of a child?

Part 1:
Introduction

At the start of the narrative the author is three years old. Characters and events are seen with a child's sense of wonder and bewilderment. This poses an exciting challenge for the author; to recreate the world in an authentic child-like way.

Part 2:
An infant
world

- The young Laurie Lee crawls from place to place initially. To reflect this there is often a distorted sense of scale in descriptions, particularly of people. The sisters tower above him, legs and stockings scurry to and fro.
- Happenings are often described in an abrupt way. The world is unpredictable to a toddler with no clear sense of time.
- A child's needs outweigh larger events in the adult world. The security of having his mother with him, sleep, food, immediate concerns, affects the child in a way that war or an end to it do not.
- Strong emotions, such as jealously, injustice, irritation, often colour accounts of events.

Part 3:
Growth and
experience

- As Laurie Lee grows in experience and becomes increasingly mobile he begins to learn new tricks and make exciting discoveries.
- The child's curiosity increases and accounts begin to emphasise this urge to question, experiment and explore.

- He is suddenly more observant, astute to changes in the seasons and in himself.

Part 4:
Language

- Language in the early sections is often deliberately childlike.
- We get a sense of a child relying on grown-ups for opinions, 'he was a soldier, because Mother had said so' (p. 19), or making bold but rather naïve assertions, 'I knew about war, all my uncles were in it' (p. 19).
- A child's lack of certainty often emerges through the author's choice of language.

Part 5:
Styles of
narrative

- Sometimes characters and events are exaggerated reflecting a child's lack of experience. A downpour becomes a life-threatening event because our narrator is so young.
- Characters are often polarised into heroes and villains. Laurie Lee selects events that depict his uncles as action heroes but we sense his uneasiness in descriptions of local figures like Albert the Devil.
- Some stories are related with the partial understanding of a child in mind. Young Laurie Lee finds it hard to grasp the soldier's predicaments, even envies him for being able to sleep in the woods but is confused when his sisters tell him that the police have taken the man away 'in a cart'.
- Comical misunderstandings underline an infant's lack of experience. At school the author is annoyed at not receiving the promised 'present' (p. 44).

Part 6:
A child's
imagination

- The writer skilfully selects those memories that had the greatest impact on his imagination as a boy.
- Tales of a sinister or disturbing nature predominate.

Part 7:
Author as a
young man

- In the later sections the author as a teenager begins to appreciate the complexities of life.
- He witnesses the courtship of his sisters, the eventual fragmentation of his own family.

- Along with his peers he struggles to come to terms with new urges and impulses of his own.

Part 8:
Conclusion

Laurie Lee's account of childhood, growth and development is fresh and inventive. We are tempted to recall moments from our own childhood through the author's vivid use of language and skilful selection of events.

FURTHER QUESTIONS

Make a plan as shown above and attempt these questions.

1 How does Laurie Lee use language to create vivid impressions of people and places?

2 Laurie Lee has different feelings for his mother and father. How are these two characters depicted in the story?

3 Which episodes best illustrate the nature of village life? Choose any one incident and explain what we learn about Slad and the valley, from it?

4 Writing *Cider with Rosie* was an attempt to 'live again both the good and the bad'. Choose two incidents from Laurie Lee's childhood that illustrate positive and negative aspects of his upbringing.

5 Sections of the book are memorable for their humour. Which episode do you find amusing and why?

6 Shortly after her arrival in Slad imagine that Mrs Lee writes a letter to her estranged husband. Write her letter explaining the difficulties she now faces and the situation she finds herself in.

7 Write an account about the Lee household from the perspective of a near neighbour.

8 Which characters from the story leave the most vivid impression on you? Choose two and explain what interests you about them.

PART FIVE

CULTURAL CONNECTIONS

BROADER PERSPECTIVES

A good starting point for a fuller understanding of Laurie Lee's craft is the collection of writings under the title, *I Can't Stay Long* (Penguin Books, Harmondsworth, 1975). Among essays about his many travels is a piece on the subject of writing **autobiography** (see Literary Terms) where Laurie Lee outlines some of the problems he encountered and his aims and overall intention.

Cider with Rosie could be studied in conjunction with film versions, concentrating on ways in which the text has been adapted and edited for the screen. Hugh Whitemore's screenplay of 'Cider with Rosie' (1993, BBCV 4462) starred Rosemary Leach and the author made an appearance as his older self. A recent adaptation by John Mortimer for ITV (1999, Carlton Home Video 3007401753) featured Juliet Stevenson as Laurie Lee's mother and incorporated the voice of Laurie Lee in its commentary.

Alternatively, the many episodes in Laurie Lee's early life lend themselves to a media project where a selection of the text could be scripted alongside a storyboard for a television episode.

When Laurie Lee died, aged 83, on 13 May 1997, local and national newspapers published a variety of articles on the writer's life and work. Obituaries detail his many achievements and offer a modern perspective on his writing.

A study of *Cider with Rosie* could be linked with the novel *To Kill a Mockingbird* by Harper Lee (Minerva, 1991 – first published 1960). Although the story takes place in America during the depression, both depict childhood in a small and narrow rural community. The novel explores the theme of prejudice in America's Deep South but it also dramatises the children's growth through experience.

Laurie Lee used his autobiography to plot the slow death of country traditions. Thomas Hardy wrote novels, short stories and poetry with similar themes in mind. He too uses a range of rustic characters to help tell his tales of rural Wessex and was sceptical about the new ideas and mechanisation threatened by the Industrial Revolution. In *The Mayor of Casterbridge* (Heinemann, 1993 – first published 1886), Michael Henchard's eventual ruin is set against major upheavals in society.

LITERARY TERMS

autobiography a prose account of ones own life

image / imagery use of language to create a picture in the readers mind to suggest feelings or make comparisons for us

irony moments where we have a sense of the writer saying one thing but meaning something altogether different

narrative the style in which the story is told

rustic chorus minor characters from rural life who are allowed to comment briefly on action or events in the story

setting place where the story happens

TEST ANSWERS

TEST YOURSELF (Chapter 1)

A 1 Laurie Lee *(Chapter 1)*
2 Sisters *(Chapter 1)*
3 Mother *(Chapter 1)*
4 Deserting soldier *(Chapter 1)*
5 Father *(Chapter 1)*

TEST YOURSELF (Chapters 2–4)

A 1 Mother *(Chapter 2)*
2 Albert the Devil *(Chapter 2)*
3 Spadge Hopkins *(Chapter 3)*
4 Laurie Lee at Junior School *(Chapter 3)*
5 Marjorie *(Chapter 4)*

TEST YOURSELF (Chapters 5–10)

A 1 Granny Wallon *(Chapter 5)*
2 Fred Bates *(Chapter 6)*
3 Mr Jolly, the Schoolmaster *(Chapter 7)*

4 The old Squire *(Chapter 8)*
5 Vincent returned from New Zealand *(Chapter 6)*

TEST YOURSELF (Chapters 11–12)

A 1 Dorothy in fancy dress *(Chapter 11)*
2 The Squire *(Chapter 11)*
3 Jo, Laurie Lee's girlfriend *(Chapter 12)*
4 Rosie Burdock *(Chapter 12)*
5 Walt Kerry the bully *(Chapter 12)*

TEST YOURSELF (Chapter 13)

A 1 Old Mrs Clissold *(Chapter 13)*
2 Maurice, Marjorie's boyfriend *(Chapter 13)*
3 Mother on the picnic *(Chapter 13)*
4 Laurie Lee *(Chapter 13)*
5 The village's old folk *(Chapter 13)*

Notes

OTHER TITLES

GCSE and equivalent levels (£3.50 each)

Maya Angelou
I Know Why the Caged Bird Sings

Jane Austen
Pride and Prejudice

Alan Ayckbourn
Absent Friends

Elizabeth Barrett Browning
Selected Poems

Robert Bolt
A Man for All Seasons

Harold Brighouse
Hobson's Choice

Charlotte Brontë
Jane Eyre

Emily Brontë
Wuthering Heights

Shelagh Delaney
A Taste of Honey

Charles Dickens
David Copperfield

Charles Dickens
Great Expectations

Charles Dickens
Hard Times

Charles Dickens
Oliver Twist

Roddy Doyle
Paddy Clarke Ha Ha Ha

George Eliot
Silas Marner

George Eliot
The Mill on the Floss

William Golding
Lord of the Flies

Oliver Goldsmith
She Stoops To Conquer

Willis Hall
The Long and the Short and the Tall

Thomas Hardy
Far from the Madding Crowd

Thomas Hardy
The Mayor of Casterbridge

Thomas Hardy
Tess of the d'Urbervilles

Thomas Hardy
The Withered Arm and other Wessex Tales

L.P. Hartley
The Go-Between

Seamus Heaney
Selected Poems

Susan Hill
I'm the King of the Castle

Barry Hines
A Kestrel for a Knave

Louise Lawrence
Children of the Dust

Harper Lee
To Kill a Mockingbird

Laurie Lee
Cider with Rosie

Arthur Miller
The Crucible

Arthur Miller
A View from the Bridge

Robert O'Brien
Z for Zachariah

Frank O'Connor
My Oedipus Complex and other stories

George Orwell
Animal Farm

J.B. Priestley
An Inspector Calls

Willy Russell
Educating Rita

Willy Russell
Our Day Out

J.D. Salinger
The Catcher in the Rye

William Shakespeare
Henry IV Part 1

William Shakespeare
Henry V

William Shakespeare
Julius Caesar

William Shakespeare
Macbeth

William Shakespeare
The Merchant of Venice

William Shakespeare
A Midsummer Night's Dream

William Shakespeare
Much Ado About Nothing

William Shakespeare
Romeo and Juliet

William Shakespeare
The Tempest

William Shakespeare
Twelfth Night

George Bernard Shaw
Pygmalion

Mary Shelley
Frankenstein

R.C. Sherriff
Journey's End

Rukshana Smith
Salt on the snow

John Steinbeck
Of Mice and Men

Robert Louis Stevenson
Dr Jekyll and Mr Hyde

Jonathan Swift
Gulliver's Travels

Robert Swindells
Daz 4 Zoe

Mildred D. Taylor
Roll of Thunder, Hear My Cry

Mark Twain
Huckleberry Finn

James Watson
Talking in Whispers

William Wordsworth
Selected Poems

A Choice of Poets

Mystery Stories of the Nineteenth Century including The Signalman

Nineteenth Century Short Stories

Poetry of the First World War

Six Women Poets

York Notes Advanced (£3.99 each)

Margaret Atwood
The Handmaid's Tale

Jane Austen
Mansfield Park

Jane Austen
Persuasion

Jane Austen
Pride and Prejudice

Alan Bennett
Talking Heads

William Blake
Songs of Innocence and of Experience

Charlotte Brontë
Jane Eyre

Emily Brontë
Wuthering Heights

Geoffrey Chaucer
The Franklin's Tale

Geoffrey Chaucer
General Prologue to the Canterbury Tales

Geoffrey Chaucer
The Wife of Bath's Prologue and Tale

Joseph Conrad
Heart of Darkness

Charles Dickens
Great Expectations

John Donne
Selected Poems

George Eliot
The Mill on the Floss

F. Scott Fitzgerald
The Great Gatsby

E.M. Forster
A Passage to India

Brian Friel
Translations

Thomas Hardy
The Mayor of Casterbridge

Thomas Hardy
Tess of the d'Urbervilles

Seamus Heaney
Selected Poems from Opened Ground

Nathaniel Hawthorne
The Scarlet Letter

James Joyce
Dubliners

John Keats
Selected Poems

Christopher Marlowe
Doctor Faustus

Arthur Miller
Death of a Salesman

Toni Morrison
Beloved

William Shakespeare
Antony and Cleopatra

William Shakespeare
As You Like It

William Shakespeare
Hamlet

William Shakespeare
King Lear

William Shakespeare
Measure for Measure

William Shakespeare
The Merchant of Venice

William Shakespeare
Much Ado About Nothing

William Shakespeare
Othello

William Shakespeare
Romeo and Juliet

William Shakespeare
The Tempest

William Shakespeare
The Winter's Tale

Mary Shelley
Frankenstein

Alice Walker
The Color Purple

Oscar Wilde
The Importance of Being Earnest

Tennessee Williams
A Streetcar Named Desire

John Webster
The Duchess of Malfi

W.B. Yeats
Selected Poems